Pawnshop on Monday
Sheffield Folk Remember

Edited by
Margaret Rutherford
and M. Christine Bolsover

PAWNSHOP ON MONDAY

SHEFFIELD FOLK REMEMBER

EDITED BY
MARGARET RUTHERFORD
AND
M. CHRISTINE BOLSOVER

The **Hallamshire** Press
1994

Copyright © 1994, 1995 Margaret Rutherford and M. Christine Bolsover

First published by The Hallamshire Press 1994
Reprinted 1995
The Hallamshire Press is an imprint of
Interleaf Productions Limited
Exchange Works
Sidney Street
Sheffield S1 3QF
England

Typeset by Interleaf Productions Limited
Printed in Great Britain by
The Cromwell Press, Wiltshire

British Library Cataloguing in Publication Data
  Pawnshop on Monday: Sheffield Folk Remember
    I. Rutherford, Margaret II. Bolsover, M.
    Christine
    942.821082092

  ISBN 1-874718-03-2

Contents

Acknowledgements

Pawnshop on Monday is the result of a project that ran from 1991 to 1994 in Coleridge House, part of Community Health Sheffield and situated in the grounds of the Northern General Hospital.

Many people played a part in the project, and thanks are due to all of them. In particular I would like to the thank the patients who were interviewed, and the staff of Coleridge House, especially Sister Maureen Ibbotson and Sister Joy Coope. Susan Western and Barbara Rodgers of the Northern General Patients Library have been extremely helpful.

My thanks also go to Betty Dickinson, who says exactly the right things in her introduction; to the Central Library Word Processing Unit; the Local Studies Library and Mick Spick; the Off The Shelf Festival team; and Jill Leeming. My grateful appreciation is extended to Bill Bucklow of Firth Park Library Computer Club for all his hard work; to Pauline Climpson and the staff of The Hallamshire Press, who published this collection, for their support.

Finally, an incredible amount of work has been done by Margaret Rutherford and Christine Bolsover in working on the interviews, transcribing them, keeping the flavour of the originals in their editing, and being patient and tolerant of all the delays and mistakes that occurred during the project. Without Margaret and Christine there would have been no book, so many, many thanks to them for their time, toil, sweat and tears!

Keith Morris (Consultant Editor)
Patients Library Service
Sheffield Libraries

Introduction

I welcome the opportunity to write an introduction to this extraordinary, fascinating collection of memories contributed by elderly patients at Coleridge House—a vital part of the community of the Northern General Hospital.

The caring staff at Coleridge create the right atmosphere to encourage this kind of project, whilst Christine Bolsover and Margaret Rutherford, both retired librarians, who actually conducted the interviews, possess the necessary mixture of patience, understanding and humour which puts people at ease.

Amongst the contributors to this novel collection of anecdotes are a former table-knife buffer, the son of an old fashioned street-lamp lighter and a jolly lady who openly admits that at fourteen years old, she was 'too fat to play games'.

Tales of the 'depression' crop up quite often, together with Banners cheques, Spirella corsets and our beloved tramcars—well, they couldn't leave those out, could they?

A wartime pilot of Lancaster Bombers tells of his exploits; whilst playing truant from school and playing football for Sheffield Wednesday all take their part.

Happy summer picnics in Endcliffe and Millhouses parks and day excursions to Skegness and Mablethorpe are recalled with nostalgic pleasure.

This book will awaken happy memories for the older generation but it will also be a revelation, maybe even an education, for younger readers.

Betty Dickinson
author of SHANTY TOWN 1985
DAHN T'VILLAGE TO WINCOBANK 1990
NEVER FAR FROM WINCOBANK 1992

Betsy Baines
(Aged 67)

Holey breadcakes!

We used to live on Petre Street. They were only terrace-type houses and going up to them was a great big open archway. The houses belonged to Wilds the fish people and one family of Wilds lived in our yard, they had eight children.

The mother used to bake every day. She made these breadcakes with all holes in and I used to think they were beautiful—oven bottom cakes. My mother always made breadcakes and she did 'em properly. Everybody liked her breadcakes but me, it was ever so funny. If mother said, 'Do you want a breadcake?' I used to say 'No, I'll go and have one of Mrs. Wild's'. I think it was because of all the holes in them and the butter used to run into the holes.

A fishy tale

There were big garages in our yard and Wilds used to bring their fish vans up and park them there. They had a shop on Spital Hill, a stall in the market and a shop up the gennel at Firth Park. Everybody used to go for Wild's fish. They used to go every week, the Wild's vans, into Lincolnshire to fetch chickens, rabbits and eggs—they used to stamp eggs with their own name, it was real interesting. They used to come back with all these rabbits and that. It used to be a brace of rabbits for 1/6d, two chickens for a little bit more, but I can't remember just what. All the neighbours used to have them, we lived on rabbit and chicken for ages after. If they broke any eggs when they were stamping them, they used to put them in a big basin and you got those for nothing! We were glad we lived near Wilds. Now we've brought all these memories back I can just see them, stamping those eggs in the big garage. We used to think it was fascinating, and watching them break eggs and putting them in a basin at the side. We had custards, no end of custards, when there were all those broken eggs. In the family of Wilds in our yard was the brother of the one who owned the shops—Walter Wild—they were a real nice family.

It was a real laugh

Every so often there used to be an organ-grinder come round and he used to leave his organ in our yard—it was a very big yard. My dad was a very small man and he used to pretend to be the monkey on the top and my brother used to be winding the organ. People used to come from all over to watch. It was a real laugh—a performance! It was really my earliest memory of anything, I can see that organ now—it was ever so funny.

Going up in the world

My dad worked down at Firth Brown's and Mr Firth was a real down to earth man. Dad worked in an office on his own, Mr Firth came and asked him if he'd like to go and work for him at Dore, but at his house and be gardener. I can see Mum and Dad now, talking it over, anyway they decided to go. I thought, Dore! I'd never been to Dore, and so we went to live there. We had some really happy times. We'd a great big tree in the garden with a swing on it. All the family, cousins and that, used to come up on a Sunday and we'd have tea on the lawn, swing on the tree and all sorts of things. It was called something Croft Cottage and was right opposite the green. I think the cottage has gone now and they've built some new houses there. Our house was right next to the War Memorial.

Mr and Mrs Firth left and went to Scotland, the right north of Scotland. They asked my dad if he'd go with them, but he said no, he wouldn't go right up there like. So, the people that bought Kings Croft, that house, were the Batchelors—and that's another story.

Still boss and worker

It was Batchelors pea people you see. When my dad was young he lived in Jamaica Street and so did Mr Batchelor's family. Dad's family were a lot better off then than the Batchelor family. The Batchelors started their business going round from door to door with tea, and sometimes my dad used to go with the boys. When Dad went to work for him, after the Firths, he recognised Mr Batchelor straight away. Oh yes, Dad knew who he was but he didn't say anything. But, Mr Maurice, as my dad called him, said, 'I know you from years ago, don't I?' Then he thought a bit and said, 'I know, Arthur Carter!' Of course, they got very friendly but they were still boss and worker.

I nearly died

I can allus remember when Dad worked for Batchelor's. I went part time cleaning for them, I was married by then. I was in the entrance hall where they had beautiful pictures, well you can imagine can't you? I was looking at this picture and I thought, 'That does look dirty, that picture'. So I got a leather and I'd been doing it for a bit when all of a sudden Mr Batchelor came in and he says, 'I hope you're not putting any water on that picture'. And I said, 'Oh no! Oh no!' I nearly died, it was an oil painting!

He's a nice lad!

My husband used to live in the next yard to me. I was only sixteen when I met him, we were still living in Petre Street, he was a very, very quiet person. He's not now, but he was then! He didn't go out boozing or anything, like the other lads did. 'Course that suited my Mother, she'd say, 'Oh, he's a nice lad' and all this, that and the other. So, we started going out together and ended up being married— it's very nearly fifty years now. I was twenty-one and he was twenty-three when we married. We got married in Dore church—it's a lovely church.

I bet Betsy's made this!

When I first started work I worked at Davy's, in the bakery. They had a shop at Hunter's Bar and the bakery was over it. I can't remember just how long I worked there, but it was until they closed it down and took us all to Castle

Street. I did all sorts, made pastry, buns, flaky pastry—we put that through a mangle. It was funny, the men did the heavy work which was lifting great big bowls of cream, pastry mix, bun mixture—all sorts of things. If the man who did all this heavy work was off they used to have me doing it and I was only as thin as a rail! Me and the boss used to lift these great big bowls on to a bin and weigh it all out on the scales. When I think about it I don't know how I did it, 'cos I was only a little bit of a thin thing, but it didn't make no difference to me. I started working there at fourteen when we lived at Petre Street. I had to be at Hunters Bar at seven-thirty and oh, when it was dark mornings and I had to leave home at six-thirty! I got a bus from our end and a tram from town. I worked until four-thirty. While I worked there and for years after, I couldn't eat a cream bun. The cream was like meringue stuff. They used to buy it in tins and it was jelly-like, only white. We used to mix that with cream to make it go further—so much albumen and so much cream. It's surprising, it used to say 'fresh cream' and it did have fresh cream in it, but something else to make it go further!

My mother had a friend that lived across the road in Petre Street and she'd been her friend from being a little girl. She used to buy a cream cake, or something else with cream in it, from Davy's every Saturday. If there seemed to be extra cream in it her husband used to say the same thing every time—'I bet Betsy's made this'. I think he thought I'd put extra cream in just for them.

Doris Wallace
(Aged 75)

A season's strawberry picking

One summer when I was unemployed, the people at the Labour Exchange asked if any of us wanted to go for a season's strawberry picking in Wisbech, on the borders of Cambridgeshire, Lincolnshire and Norfolk. They sent a gang of us off in a covered lorry. We were accommodated in barns where we slept on mattresses, and bought food out of the money we earned. We were paid by the punnet and it was back-aching work.

I met my husband, a Wisbech man, while I was there. I came home, got married and went back to live there for fifteen or sixteen years. My husband worked on the land

and did property repairs too. I used to go and work along-side him, helping him out. I'd do hoeing, apple picking and what not—all very hard work. It was alright living down there, but at the back of my mind I knew I wanted to come back to Sheffield because all my family was here. We lived in Lincolnshire, first at Sutton Bridge where my first son was born, and then in Walpole St Andrew where my two other sons and my daughter were born.

I remember coming back to Sheffield for a visit after I'd been there a few years, bringing my eldest son with me. I'd just got the one child at that time. I listened to every-body talking, and thought to myself, 'Have I ever talked like that?' I think that my accent had changed, but down there in Norfolk they all knew I was Yorkshire.

Left me with a bucket and some string

In about 1937 we moved into a brand new council house—first tenants. Anyway, my husband went off to work and I didn't even know where to get the water from. He'd just left me a bucket and some string! There was what was called a cistern out in the back yard, and you had to get water up from it, like from a well. Anyhow, I went out with the bucket and luckily some new neighbours noticed me and came to help. But, because the house was new and there hadn't been much rain, there was hardly any water so the council brought me a load of water in a tank and poured it in the cistern.

There was no electricity or gas either so we had to use paraffin lamps, moving from room to room with them. I had to cook over the fire on a range, smaller than a York-shire range, but good enough. To do the washing I had to fetch water up into the wash-house and boil it. It was very hard work. Before I moved to Norfolk I'd been living on the Manor Estate where we'd had gas, electricity and hot and cold water all laid on.

If we needed a doctor we had to go four miles. I've had a bad leg all my life—osteomylitis—and in those days we had to pay doctor's bills. One year I remember having to go apple picking to earn the money.

The farmers provided lorries

As for shopping, well most of it was brought to the door. The baker came three times a week and the butcher called too. The nearest place for clothes and so on was Wisbech and we'd go by pushbike. Twice a week on market days, which were Wednesdays and Saturdays, there'd be a bus but we didn't go often. When we did it would be a real outing. Every Tuesday there was a bus to King's Lynn, which was a bit further, and if you went there it was for a special day out. The nearest proper seaside place was Hunstanton where the children went for their annual Sunday School outing. The farmers provided lorries and drivers, and we put charabanc-type seats in the back. When it rained there was a canopy to sit under. We parents used to go as well and took a picnic with us.

The village in winter

In the village it was very dark outside in winter as there were no gas lamps or any sort of lighting in the streets. I remember doing a lot of sewing and knitting on those winter evenings. The children would play outside, but you'd only to shout them and they'd hear you. You never wondered where they were as you knew they'd be close by, although

I did worry about them playing in haystacks as they could fall and it was a long way to the doctor's. During the dark evenings they showed films in the village hall, often Tarzan ones. The children used to copy what they'd seen at these shows and there were plenty of trees for them to swing from!

Bob Thorpe
(Aged 65)

Holidays

We'd nowt, but we always went away for a day to Blackpool, Cleethorpes, Whitby—somewhere handy. Eric, Gordon, me and our Annie used to go by excursion train at about seven or eight in the morning, and it'd always be late at night when we got home. We'd take sandwiches and a flask, but do you know? I never supped tea or coffee, I liked milk, and usually had Bovril at home.

The railway

I had been left school six months when I began work on the railway. I started on number taking. As the wagons came in from Firth Brown and them places, you had to get their number as they were only allowed to stay for so many days. You wrote the time and the day on the side, and then charged them demerits for taking space up if they stayed too long. When I was doing this job, just taking numbers, I used to have a library book with me and while I was waiting for the train to come through I'd be reading.

In the Navy

In March 1940 when I was seventeen and a half, I volunteered for the Navy. I didn't think about it first—I just went.

My mother didn't like it but she just had to lump it once I was in. So did I! I was seasick every time I had to go on board. Do you know what my first meal was in the Navy? Porridge and kippers—couldn't stand 'em! There were no stabilisers on a destroyer and it was like going on the Shamrock. I didn't like it, I'm telling you the truth. I was too well looked after at home and I had to look after myself when I was in Malta. I had a good mother, t'owd lass, she's not here now . . . I left the Navy after two years, as a class B reserve, to go back to the railway.

Back with the railways

I went back to the railways in 1942 and stayed thirty odd years. First I was a messenger boy, then I went on the horses and carts and then on the lorries. I worked my way up. By the time I retired I was trunking to Stoke, what they call the Five Towns, for the National Carriers on Brightside Lane, before it burnt down. I liked driving, and I used to love going to work but then bad health overtook me. I had a tumour at the back of my eyes which they took out, and I lost my sight. Since then I've had a stroke and I can't walk at all. But I've got a good memory and I can go back years and years.

Ellen (Nellie) Ward
(Aged 75)

Games in the school yard

I was born in Owlerton, in the Bassets area. Then we went to live up at Hillsborough on Leader Road, it runs into Dykes Hall Road, I was happy living in that area. I went to Parkside Road School, in fact it was the only school I ever went to. You just carried on 'til you left, you didn't have to transfer to another school, I left at fourteen.

I was too fat, love, to play any games. It's true! I'm not kidding you, I were a plump little thing. If I'd have gone skipping they'd have sued my mother for the hole in the ground! We weren't a plump family, there was only really me. My sister was three years older than me and she was like a streak of lightning. My teacher sent word to my mother and asked if I were getting all the food and she was doing without. My mother was going to strangle her for asking! I didn't eat a lot. I wasn't barred from anything, but I wasn't greedy. My sister could eat more than me really. Mother was small but she wasn't what you could call fat and my father was tall and thin. My dad used to say that I took after his brother 'cos he was a well-made man. I was the fattest in the class. I was upset about that at first, but then they all knew me and I got used to it. I once came home from school heartbroke. You know when the doctor and nurse used to come round and give you a little check-up?

Well, she turned round and said 'It's no use you getting on the scales, we don't want them breaking'. I said to my mother when I got home, 'I'm not going to that school no more'. I never forgot that, it's always stuck with me. They put me on a diet at one time, but it made no difference. Mother cut me down on sweets, but then they found out it was what some people used to call a Derbyshire neck and that turned out to mean a goitre throat and that was what was doing it. I'm thinner now than I've ever been and I can't say I'm thin now! The only time I look thin is when I've got my corsets on!

We had a nice back yard—we used to play there. I allus remember the man next door knocking to us, we were all playing together with only a tennis ball. It just touched the window, it didn't bang it. So he comes out, man next door, and he's banging on't window and he goes and busts it! It's true, I'm not making it up. We all stood and laughed. That's always stuck in my mind whenever I see someone tapping on a window.

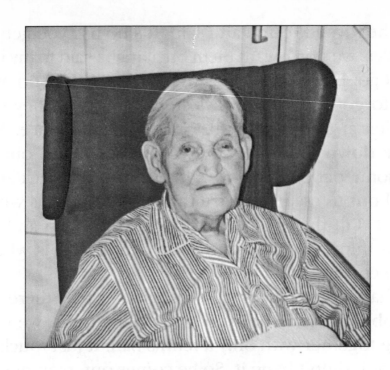

Marshall Howe
(Aged 93)

Apprentice armature winder

In 1914, when I was fourteen, I left school and went straight into the works. I was serving my time as an apprentice armature winder when war broke out and for some reason the firm then transferred the electrical part to Attercliffe Common. The firm was Vickers, but they started to call the electrical section Metropolitan Vickers. Because of the war I was held back from learning my trade. This was for the simple reason that they brought girls in to do some men's jobs and used to call on me to come back to do the coil winding which the girls couldn't do. So I missed a lot of my training. Then in the end they seemed to transfer the work to Trafford Park in Manchester, and I was out of a job three years after the war. You see I hadn't really got a trade 'cos I hadn't finished my winding apprenticeship.

'Not getting away with that'

Anyway, I had a sister-in-law who worked as secretary to a Mr Fuller in the electrical department at Cockaynes, the department store. Through her I got a job there receiving goods delivered, and booking stuff in and out to the electricians. They'd take materials from the store when they went on a job, which I'd book out, and then when they came back I'd book in what they returned. But when I was about twenty or twenty-one we got a new director, a council leader I remember, and they cut staff including me. Anyway it was an awkward time, but Mr Fuller said 'He's not getting away with that. Do you think you can do electrical wiring work?' I said 'I think so, I'll have a go at it'. So I went on a job, just up Campo Lane, where they needed a few lights doing and that was my first job.

Self-taught

After that I went all over the place working for dozens of customers all over Sheffield, and I must have been satisfactory because some of them used to ask for me specially. I didn't really have any training—I was self-taught. I used to buy books and read it up, and when I had a bit of spare time on the booking-in job, I used to practise little circuits with old wire. All in all I was there forty years, working in the Cathedral for instance and schools such as Woodthorpe.

Irene Green
(Aged 71)

I can still remember our Co-op number

We got married at Firth Park Methodist Church in 1946. Reverend Edmundson was the minister then. I wore a long white dress and we had a week's honeymoon in Scarborough. I even managed enough coupons to get a green costume to go away in. Father was a cabinet maker and so when we got married he made us a sideboard as a wedding present. We've still got it—mind you it's a bit knocked about now. We were lucky because we weren't married very long before we got a house. It was on Gray Street, at the top of Andover Street in Pitsmoor. Uncle was an estate agent and got it for us. It wasn't in a very good district, but it was a house to start us off. Then we moved to Hunter Road, Hillsborough, which is where we still are. We've kept it because it's on the flat, there's a good shopping centre and it's not far to Rivelin. It's not a big house, just two rooms with two upstairs and an attic, but big enough to bring up five children.

I went to that same church as a girl and joined the Home Fire Girls with Mrs Pryor as leader. I enjoyed going and took part in the May Queen Festivals although I was never May Queen. I remember Whit Mondays too, when we used to go and sing in Firth Park. We used to buy a bouncing ball from Kenyon's toy shop in Bellhouse Road—there was always a stall of toys outside on that day—and it wasn't Whit Monday if we didn't have a ball. It was one of those on a long string that you put on your finger. We had new clothes for Whit Monday too. Usually it was a new dress and shoes and socks. We'd go and show them off to relatives and neighbours and if we were lucky they'd sometimes give us some coppers or a threepenny bit. Often our Whit things were bought at the Co-op at Page Hall and then we'd get 'dividend' on them. I can still remember our Co-op number.

Hilda Hatton

(Aged 90)

It was all plugs and handles

I started work as a telephonist at the Sheffield Independent at 21 Fargate. They trained me—it was all plugs and handles. The job was quite good but I only got about five shillings a week. The Independent closed down eventually and I was transferred. Meanwhile, I'd been learning shorthand and typing, first at the De Bear School and then at Whiteley's College. My parents paid for me to go to Whiteley's College, they weren't well off, but they managed. So I went as a typist to Hadfield's on Newhall Road, and to their East Hecla works at Tinsley. Because it was wartime, and I was in a reserved occupation, I couldn't leave Hadfield's as soon as I would like to have done. Anyway, as soon as I could, I got another job issuing ration books in the Food Office in Carver Street, and later I worked at the National Assistance Office on Dodd Street.

I've still got that hat

I met my husband at Hadfield's. He was a clerical officer in another department but we'd always go to the dining room for lunch together, and spend break times with each other too. When we were courting we used to go to the picture houses a lot and we always went out for meals. We loved eating out, and you see, before we were married there was no one at home to cook for either of us. One day after work we went to Rotherham to buy my engagement ring and celebrated with a meal out.

When I got married, at Carver Street, I wore a really pretty suit made of fawn material with a gold streak in it, and a little rose coloured hat—I've still got that hat. It was only a small wedding, not an elaborate affair, and my brother gave me away. We went to a restaurant for the reception, but we didn't have a honeymoon, just went back to Crookes where we had a house.

During the Blitz, we were having a meal in the Cinema House when the sirens went and we all had to get out. The Montgomery Hall on Surrey Street was the nearest place with a shelter underneath and we ran in there. After the 'all clear' went we walked up Division Street to get to Crookes. We weren't married then, but we both lived in the same district. That night of the Blitz and the devastation we saw was a very frightening experience.

Joseph William Hirst

(Aged 88)

Lead in my shoes

When I was young I used to run at little handicap races all over Sheffield. They used to have races at Hyde Park Stadium, the Pheasant Inn down Attercliffe, the Ball Inn, which became a training ground for Sheffield United, and other places as well. I used to run for my uncle. He was a runner himself until he was injured in the war and lost the use of one arm—that lost his balance. We won money, not cups. They were up to all sorts of tricks, 'cos it was bookies you know. In them days there were bookies in every back yard. No, I wasn't that sort of bookie's runner! If he wanted me to win, I won, and if I knew the money wasn't on, I didn't run. Well, not to win. I was ruled by the bookies, there was a lot of that in those days. That's why he put lead in my shoes! If I was being watched, I was putting the effort in but not winning. That was rife in those days. Mind you, nobody really made much money, there wasn't much about. The average wage was about seventeen bob a week for men.

Lovely penny pies

We had a piano at home and my dad was a pianist in a pub. He played for his Buffalo Lodge too. He died at thirty-five, leaving six or seven of us at home. Mother went out to work and delegated us all a job. I had the cellar steps to clean and the half of the cellar with the coal. I became such a dab hand at this business that I used to do the bins for other people as well, and sometimes they'd give me a penny or a ha'penny for a bit of pocket money. I used to love to spend it going to the music hall. First house at the Empire and then on to the second house at the Hippo-drome. Coming home there was a shop on South Street where they made the most lovely pies—penny pies with beautiful gravy. You could go inside and watch her making them.

It's very rare I went on a tramcar, except to Endcliffe Park in the holidays. It was only a ha'penny on the tram, but we used to walk and run and save the fare and that would buy us an ice cream. We didn't worry about wearing our shoes out. They were usually ladies' shoes, often my grandmother's cast-offs with buttons up the side! We got used to wearing that sort of thing.

Gaoled for playing football

I was once arrested, taken to the police station, and spent the night there. I was playing football on a Sunday afternoon with a sixpenny ball and about half a dozen other boys. I remember the fellow who picked me up. His name was Ellerley. He took me to the police station and charged me with obstructing the footpath and playing football in the street. I was only very young at the time, about seven or eight years, but they took me in front of the magistrate next day. The lady magistrate asked me if I pleaded guilty to playing football and I said 'Yes Ma'am'. She fined me five shillings. My Father said 'Let him stop, it'll do him good', but my grandma heard about it and came and paid the five shillings. I was the only one who got caught. I could have outrun any of them, but I bumped into a little girl as we ran off and down she went. I stopped to pick her up and that was me caught. I remember asking the man, 'Aren't you Sergeant Ellerley?' He said 'Yes', but he wasn't in uniform. If he'd said he was a policeman I wouldn't have run away. I told him that my bad days were over, my father had made sure of that—he'd threatened me with a thrashing, and I mean a thrashing, if I didn't toe the line. Do you know that charge was still on my record years later when I went for an interview for a commission in the Royal Air Force. I didn't mention it at the interview, but a few days later they called me back and asked me why not. I said, 'Surely the sins of a child can't be held against him when he gets to manhood.'—They liked that answer.

No sick pay then

There was a scheme brought out at that time whereby you sat an exam called a school leaving examination. If you

32

could find someone to give you a job, you could leave the term before you were fourteen. That meant that at thirteen I was working full time in the rolling mills at Thomas Firth's on Weedon Street, handling billets heavier than myself, because I never had any meat, I was always thin. My starting wage was four and sixpence a week. I used to catch a tram on Sheaf Street to go to work. I'd run into town from home and if I missed the tram I'd set off running again and usually catch it up round Norfolk Bridge. I didn't do much other running when I'd once started work, I was too tired. We worked from six in the morning until five at night, that was on days, but on nights it was five o'clock until six next morning.

The rolling mills never stopped during the 1914–18 war. I had an accident, I was working on a machine which used to straighten a bar when it came from the mill. I had to push it up a tube which was only half an inch bigger than the diameter of the bar. This particular bar was very bent and I pushed and pushed then I slipped and fell over it—it was red hot and I was badly burnt. I spent three or four months in hospital, but I survived. No sick pay or compensation then though.

And Mother came too

Later, I worked on the trams, I started as a conductor. How did I meet my wife? Well, I was on duty one morning on Bramall Lane. We pulled up near her home, though I didn't know that at the time, and I heard this pitter-patter, pitter-patter of ladies' shoe heels and so I waited until she appeared. She had the most beautiful garters! She went upstairs and I went up after her to collect her fare, and I told her so! I said, 'Your garters are lovely' and she snubbed me. I told her that I had waited so she could catch the tram and she said, 'Yes, but you didn't wait for my dad'. We'd left him behind! The next morning she was there again, but so was her dad. Anyway, I dated her. We arranged to meet at the tram stop in the Wicker and she turned up, but so did her mother. I ended up taking both of them to the pictures! We used to take her mother in the circle at the Coliseum on Spital Hill, but not every time. She thought I was a nice lad. I went to their house but her old man wasn't there, so I asked her mother about courting. She said, 'You'll have to ask Father, not me'. Anyway, I knew where he worked and he was a walking man, walked home from work up Sutherland Road. One day I met him and put my case to him. He said, 'Well, tha looks all reight lad. Ah tha working?' I said, 'Yes, I work on the trams'. 'That's OK, if tha looks after that tha's got a job for life'. And I had—I worked on them for thirty-eight years. We got married on a Sunday. Actually, I arranged it because that Sunday was my day off. We married at Sale Memorial Church and I was working again the next day.

Tom Disbury

(Aged 71)

Town Crier

Before the war I belonged to the Don Variety Players, and I remember being a Town Crier in a production we did at the Bellhouse Road Club. I still know the words to a lot of the songs we did and I like to sing them if anyone wants to listen. But, I've always stammered a lot when I talk. It upset me when I was young, and when I went shopping for my mother to get her a loaf or something, she used to give me a note.

Stuart Smith

(Aged 80)

Always in uniform

I was born in Dykes Hall Road and went to Malin Bridge Council School from five to fourteen. Then I had to start work and the funny thing about this is, I've been in uniform almost all my working life.

Buttons, never boots

My first job was as a page boy, or buttons as they called them, at the Angel Hotel in Angel Street. It's not there now, but it used to be just below the old Cockaynes Arcade. It was a temperance hotel and had lots of commercial travellers who stayed there overnight. We used to do a little bit on the side, fetching these men beer etc. from the old Shades, which was a pot house—the Dove and Rainbow is there now. I used to get a penny, or something like that, for bringing it in under cover. I stayed there until I got to be a boots at almost seventeen. I knew I wouldn't get much further because there was boots and second boots who'd both been there for years. I'd always wanted to be in uniform and I asked one of the commercial travellers if he'd any ideas about a job, could he find me one? 'What you want to do, son, is join the Army. Then come out of the Army and join the Police'.

In the Army now

So I went to the recruitment place on Surrey Street to apply and they asked me how old I was. I said seventeen and a half and they said, 'No you're not, you're eighteen!' 'Cos you see, he got a King's shilling. I said I wanted to go in the Cavalry but was told they were full up. So they put me in the Artillery, which then didn't mean a thing to me. The Recruitment Officer asked me what I wanted to go in for— three and nine, or, six and six. I thought he was talking about money, so I thought, 'I'll have a go at six and a tanner (six and six). It turned out that three and nine meant three in the army and nine on reserve, or, six in the army and six on reserve. I think it was deliberate saying it like that, making us think they were talking about money. Anyway, I went six and six. Then I went home and told my mother that I'd been and gone and done it and she was really mad. You see, working in the hotel she didn't have to keep me. I could give her a few bob a week and I had all my keep at the hotel. But I told her it would be the same with me in the Army and that smoothed things over.

My tattoos were in vain

I went down to Woolwich and did my basic training. After my basic training, but still before I was eighteen, I was due to be posted to India. A group of us went and had our knees tattooed, so that the tattoo would show when we were wearing our tropical kit. When my mother found out about the overseas posting, she was so upset she complained because I was under age. I was allowed to stay in the Army but not sent to India—my tattoos were in vain!

When I came to have my legs amputated I was very upset at the thought of losing my tattoos after all those years, so I told my surgeon the story. He was so interested that he promised to try and save them, which in fact he did. I think he was as pleased with his handiwork as I was.

Anyway, I eventually finished my six years and came out on reserve.

Back in uniform at last

When I first came out I applied to the police in Sheffield straight away. They wouldn't take local lads on in those days, but they gave me a medical, tested me, measured me and everything and I got in at Manchester. So, off I went to Manchester. There were thirty of us, and I finished up in the last four. Then they rejected two of us and I was one of those two. After that I tried for asylum attendant, prison warder, anything with uniform. I wanted uniform but failed. For a while I got a job travelling round calling on shops selling potted meat for Binghams. I was courting then, court-ing my wife and this was in 1938, the year we got married. Then I tried for the buses—more uniform! After quite a spell of calling in to see the Personnel Officer I eventually got on at the beginning of 1939 as a driver.

I'll never forget that Captain

Later that year, 1939, war was declared and I was still on reserve with one year to do. As early as May that year, they were calling reservists back for a few months' refresher course and then sending them home again. I fell for the August batch and never got back home. War was declared on September 3rd, by the 18th I had landed in Brest as part of a road party, I was a driver then. We went here, there and everywhere and had to find our own billets if we could, or sleep in the wagon. Then the balloon went up. We went into Belgium and Holland and got our bottoms smacked as you know, and then it was retreat, retreat, retreat. We had a Captain in charge of us, Captain Bevan, he lined us all up under a hedgerow. All the roads were like the M1, everyone going to Dunkirk, and he left us there under that hedgerow, waiting, waiting, while he went to reconnoitre a route to get us there. I'll never forget that Captain, he took us a tortuous route, but we licked them to it. He got us all onto the beaches. I've often wondered, many and many a day, about the Beachmaster who lined us all up. What became of him? We were getting away and he was still there organising everyone. When I finally got aboard, —I went into the water of course—I got on a Navy corvette called the Hydrangea, one of the Flower Class, and they landed us at Dover. My brother-in-law, strangely enough, served on that boat.

They didn't know I'd jumped the train

After we got back they gave us all new stuff and we were sent to Leeds to reorganise. We came up by train and when we got to Sheffield I jumped! So I went home, but of course, two or three days later I knew I just had to go back, go and report. They welcomed me with open arms! They didn't know I'd jumped the train, they thought I'd been lost at Dunkirk. They were so pleased to see me, they sent me home straight away on a fortnight's leave! How can anyone pull one as fast as that?

A nasty, nasty mob

I went right through the war, right across Europe and eventually, back again. When they came through to sign on V.E. day we were at a place called Bremervorde, between Bremer and Hamburg. We were still in action at that time and we saw all the staff-cars passing through to Luneburg Heath. From there we moved to Oldenburg. It was our job to disarm the 15th Panzer Grenadiers, but they were a nasty, nasty mob. I must admit we were a bit scared knowing who they were. They came in, lined all their vehicles up just as though they had a car park attendant directing them. Then, when we were wondering what was going to happen next, they got out, lined themselves up, and marched off.

We weren't angels

You know how we sent all our kids off to the West Country for safety, well Oldenburg was in one of the safe areas of Germany. They hadn't a window broken there—it was a revelation! One of our jobs was to guard the factories, a coffee factory for one. We were stealing it of course, and using the coffee to barter for things like Schnapps. You could even go and have your photo taken for a handful of coffee beans. We weren't angels! Oh no, no, no!

Over twenty-five years on the job

Anyway, when I was finally demobbed, I went off like everyone else for my demob suit and trilby and what have you and then went straight back to work on the buses. They made me an Inspector after a while, on the Outer Circle and then a Traffic Inspector in 1948. I was the longest serving Inspector on the job—over twenty-five years—and for the last ten of those I was what you call Senior Traffic Inspector.

Annie Hewitt

(Aged 78)

In service

At home we had two big bedrooms and this was enough for the eleven of us, because as soon as a girl was old enough she went into service. When I was in service, I got five shillings a week and my board. I'd be up at six to light the stove, and get to bed about ten pm. As a rule they'd do their own cooking and I'd wash up and so on. The work was hard and lonely and if you'd nothing else to do, you had to clean the silver. I didn't like the people I went to—both families were mean. Mean with food, mean with every-thing. I usually got Thursday off one week and Sunday the next, and I always went home. Whenever I saw a tram going to Tinsley, I'd feel very homesick and wish I was on it. I didn't like the job and always said if I'd had a dozen girls, none of them would go into service.

Yance's the jeweller's

Then I got another job through an agent on Broomhall Street. I worked as housekeeper to a jeweller's at the corner of Fitzwilliam Street and Devonshire Street, near where The Ravens pub was. When Mrs Yance saw me she said, 'I do like you. I hope you're going to come', and I said, 'The same applies, I hope I can'. I really loved her and we never had a wrong word. Her husband had been German and he'd died in a concentration camp on the Isle of Wight in the First World War. She worked in the shop and her nephew came in every day—he did the watch repairs and so on too. Just me and her lived at the back of the shop. There was a nice living room and kitchen, with two big bedrooms and an attic above. I looked after her, and did the cleaning and so on, I had two half days, Thursday and Sunday. After she'd shut the shop at night, I'd go in the back and sit with her, she was a lovely old lady and I was with her for years. She really loved me, and after I got married I still saw her as we didn't live very far away. She used to ask if my husband, Jack, was going out after tea, because if he was I'd go back up and stay with her until about nine o'clock. When I had to say 'no love, I'm not coming back tonight' she'd say 'I wish you were but it's not being fair to him to be making you come'. She was scared to death of being on her own. My husband used to keep a pig, and Mrs Yance had a lovely charm in the shape of a pig. Anyway she said, 'Give this charm to Jack, and tell him how much I appreciate him letting you come to stay with me'.

I remember the night of the Blitz. It was her new house-keeper Margaret's night off and Mrs Yance was really frightened of being on her own. She said 'I'll be so glad when it is time for Margaret to come home' and then she locked up after me. The sirens sounded soon after I'd gone—and all that corner went. There was a couple living next door who had come from Southampton and brought their little girl with them to be safe and they all got killed.

Highdays and holidays

We never went away for a week when I was young, but we'd have a day at the seaside. I loved Skegness, it was the first seaside place I ever went to and it's not changed much. We used to climb up the steps to the Victoria Station to get an early train. We also went to Blackpool Illuminations—all the lot of us. It cost five shillings then on the train and we'd take a picnic.

We never had any particular jobs to do at home, but my mother liked us to take the kids out so that she could get on with the housework. We didn't mind at all. We'd go to High Hazels Park or we'd come up Brightside Lane and up Upwell Street to Firth Park, with the little ones in the pram. We'd take something to eat and drink. Mum and Dad used to go on lots of picnics with us. We often went to Mill-houses Park too—it was only a penny to get there and a penny to get back. Sometimes we'd go to Endcliffe Park on the tram. We had some lovely times. The kids we played with used to want to come with us—as if my mother and dad hadn't got enough of their own! There were nine of us children. The kids round about—their mothers never took them out, you see. So they used to tag on with us.

Father

The reason my father was like he was, is because he lost both his parents when he was seven and he didn't know what family life was. That's what made him try to make such a good family life for all of us. His brothers and sisters took him in, and for one brother with a paper shop in Gore Street he used to deliver papers. He'd be up at five in the morning, and he used to say he'd run an errand for a slice of bread and jam. He had a hard life. His family looked after him and his sisters were good to him, but it was tough—not like it is today. As he got older, started courting and settled down, things got better. He always said that he'd had a hard life and wasn't going to let his kids have the same. My father had an accident as a boy and had half his foot taken off. Then later he got gangrene in this foot and had to have his leg off. Three years later he collapsed and died at work. He was sixty-four. Up to the time he died he used to cry when he heard 'Home Sweet Home'. I look back and think how good our parents were to us—very understanding.

Joyce Radford
(Aged 66)

Frightened of the machinery

When I left school my dad had got this job all laid on for me at Brown Bayley's as all our family worked there. It was working with Comptometers, but I didn't want to do it and in the end, a school friend of mine, Margaret, took it. Then I found my own little job at Viners the cutlers, in the Wicker. They put me to work in a big room— and oh I didn't like it. The behaviour of the people I was working with was very vulgar and my dad would have gone mad if he'd known. It really wasn't very nice, so I just kept my mouth shut and he didn't find out. I was frightened of the machinery I used for shaping knife handles, as you had to put your own stuff on it and there didn't seem to be any safety cover. In fact, I was scared every morning when I went to work, but I stuck it for a few months. I think that the manager, who was a really nice man, could see that I wasn't made for that shop. The other workers were too crude for me and I wasn't tough enough.

I really settled

Anyway the manager moved me upstairs to the etching workshop and I really settled there. Miss Clack was the Manageress, and then there was Laura, who was the main one for marking knives. My friend Dorothy Hall, from Old Hall Road, was there as well, she was two years older than me. We used to travel to and from work together and we also used to clean Viners' office together as well. I liked that because I used to love polishing things.

In the workshop we had our own machine for putting names on cutlery, like that in a printing shop. Although I started on the lowest jobs while I was learning, eventually I could do everything except Miss Clack's job. Later on we had another little girl who just wiped blades. I learnt to do etching with potash, but in spite of the windows being open the shavings got on my lungs during the three years I was there and my illness began. Another etching job, done near the stove, required very fine needles and a steady hand, but it was cleaner. Miss Clack liked to keep the workshop clean, and when we had our meals she used to get me to put tissue paper down to protect our food. Because she had duodenal ulcers she ate like a rabbit and I knew everything she had because sometimes she'd ask me to get special things for her from the Health Food Stores in Orchard Street—lettuce, nuts and demerara sugar.

The men were frightened to death

I remember Jeannie, one of the top buffers who always worked on her own. She wore a green overall and brown paper everywhere, she even wrapped it round her head like a turban, sometimes she'd come in for a chat with Miss Clack. You'd be surprised at how rough some of the other buffers could be, they were really cruel and the men were frightened to death of them. I was only a young girl and I didn't like what I saw.

I used a Dolly dye

It was while I was at Viners that I began dyeing stockings. I did them at home using a Dolly dye, dyeing odd unladdered stockings from different pairs, the same shade. I was able to get the colour even, no blotches or anything. Miss Clack had noticed how good they were and asked if I'd do them for her and my workmates, so I did them in my lunch hour. At that time some people would paint their legs and draw a seam up the back, but I never did that.

Doing a youth's job

After three years the work at Viners dropped off and my next job was at Firth Derihon on Weedon Street at Tinsley. I started at seventeen but when I was eighteen I went on to shifts, including nights, doing a youth's job as it was still wartime. I kept working until I married and would have stayed longer you know, because you had to have a very good reason for leaving in wartime, but my gran fell down the stairs and that was it. She did get better eventually but she was getting older, so I finished for good at nineteen and took over.

So much work

There was so much work to do. On Tuesdays I'd be up by four or five in the morning, putting the set pot on. I'd be washing for my grandad, grandma, me and the bairn and my husband as well before he went in the forces. I used to do the tub work, using a rubbing board, no washer then. It'd be tea-time before I'd done everything. Then I'd have the floor to do and the cellar steps, the toilet and, in summer, the place where we kept the bin. It could be nine o'clock at night before I'd done, from four in the morning.

Friday was my big downstairs cleaning day. I'd be up by four or five, black leading and everything. I finished at ten-thirty or so, and had breakfast ready for gran and grandad as I liked them to stay in bed until I'd done. Before I got married I didn't have to do a thing, but when I was married and living with them I had to do it all. Gran was not at all well by that time.

Donald Corker

(Aged 69)

Experience with a capital E

I went to Sheffield University to study Civil Engineering. I had always wanted to build a bridge but I've only been concerned with one bridge in my life. I've had a mixed life, working for quite a number of firms. My first job was during the tail end of the war when I was directed to the Royal Aircraft Establishment at Farnborough. I was doing work on aircraft undercarriages, testing new ones before they were passed for use. It was quite pleasant, with pleasant people, but it was not my ultimate wider purpose. As soon as I could leave there I joined a Civil Engineering contractor for two years, in Derbyshire. Most of the work was concerned with overland power lines and cables—the distribution of electricity. The work was relatively straight-forward and I was still young enough to be gaining experience with a capital E. After two years, I applied for a job with the Anglo-Iranian Oil Company and went out to Abu Dhabi in Persia. I worked for almost three years in a drawing office in the Air Conditioning section. This was an entirely different technical line and I learnt a lot about air conditioning and refrigeration. In due course, I came back to this country and my conditions of contract from the oil company were such that I was entitled to about five months' holiday on full pay—which was a good idea! So, I got married about a month and a half after I came back to this country. I'd met my wife before I went, she was a Sheffield girl from Bents Green. Except for six months in Middlesbrough, I spent the rest of my working life in the Sheffield area.

Rebecca Coulton
(Aged 91)

I'm one of twelve

I was born in Heage which is a little village in Derbyshire between Belper and Ripley. I'm one of twelve—three brothers and eight sisters. One day my mother felt unwell, and walked the three miles into Belper to see our own Dr Allen. She put her hands on her stomach and said 'I feel funny round here'. He said, 'Why, you're pregnant'. But she said she couldn't be because it was four years since the birth of her last child and she'd never gone that long in all her married life without becoming pregnant. 'I'll have a big family now. Oh well! I'll have to put up with it. I've done it before all those times and I've not forgotten how.' Neither of my parents came from especially large families, just five in each.

My father was a miner. They carried him out of the pit, put him to bed and ever after, although he still spent some time there, he mostly sat in a little chair at the side of the fire. On one occasion he felt worse and took to his bed, so we had to walk over to Belper to fetch the doctor. Dr Allen had no car nor trap but he did have a horse, so he rode over to our house. He came in and said 'Which of them wants me now'? My mother took him upstairs to see the patient and he took one look at my father and said 'Good God, isn't the old bugger dead yet'? My father was most offended and never had another dose of that doctor's medicine. He began making his own concoctions, his favourite being one part of laudanum to three or four parts gin. He had this four times a day

My mother used to go out papering, whitewashing and so on during the day, and then took in washing which she did two nights a week. On the other nights she did her own housework and only seemed to have two proper nights' sleep a week. But, she was always happy and cheerful, often singing to herself as she worked.

Up at 4.30

When I left school I worked in the local mill. I got up at four-thirty, leaving at five-fifteen to walk the three miles to be ready to start work at six. From eight to eight-thirty we had breakfast, lunch was between twelve and one, and work was over at five o'clock. I then had to walk back home. In winter I never saw my home or the village in daylight except during the weekends.

I was never one for going out as I much preferred to stay at home sewing and knitting for my sister's children. I wasn't interested in men or in getting married. In fact, all my life, I've never used make-up or wanted to. Now, when I was about thirty a relative heard that George Coulton, the new landlord at the Rising Sun in Ripley, was looking for a housekeeper. His wife had died four weeks before he took up the tenancy, and his parents had come with him to help him and look after his eleven-year-old son Herbert for the time being. Thinking it was all a joke I said 'Yes, fine. I can make pancakes, puddings, decorate, clean and sew as well as anyone'.

Anyway, in the end I was persuaded to try it for a few weeks. My mother said I could. I made them write a letter to the mill manager though, and he asked me if I was going pulling pints. I said no I wasn't! We were Chapel you see, and didn't go in pubs really. I got on really well with George and his parents. After I'd been there about six months some men came to see George and they had a private meeting in one of the rooms. When they had gone George said that they had given him an ultimatum, either marry or leave, all their landlords were supposed to be married.

Married on Easter Monday

Then he asked if I would consider marrying him. I thought a bit and then said 'Oh all right then'. We were married on Easter Monday and the path to the church was lined with people. Just over a year later, our son George was born and was given the second name Alan, because a friend had a son with this name and I liked it. A year or so later Dorothy Evelyn was born, Evelyn having been the name of my husband's first wife. Now I have five grandchildren and seven great-grandchildren from our family of Herbert, Alan and Dorothy. Herbert stayed with us until he married at thirty-two, so I can't have been such a bad step mother can I?

Being the landlord's wife was hard work as I had to clean the ladies' toilet and so on. We stayed in that pub thirty-two years. I loved working there. I knew all the young people, felt comfortable with them, and they seemed to like me. When we retired I remember how we moved our stuff out on the Tuesday and the new people moved theirs in on the Wednesday. As we went out, the pub was open, and people were drinking, playing darts and dominoes, and do you know, some cried because they said I'd been a good landlady and a friend to them. They said they were going to miss me, and I knew I'd miss them. We went into a bungalow near my daughter, out Derby way. Our marriage lasted nearly sixty years and we were so happy.

Robert Walker

(Aged 75)

Me dad were a lamplighter

Me dad were a lamplighter. In them days they used to go round with a thing on their shoulder. He'd push 'tap up and turn't gas on and there's a light on top and he used to light it. Depending on the time of year, in summer he'd probably go about half-past nine at night, do 'em all round West Street and all round there and then he'd go and turn them out about four in the morning. In winter he used to go about five in the afternoon and turn 'em out about eight in the morning. He used to light the lamps, turn them out and clean them. He used to clean the lamps about half-past ten in the mornings. It took him about an hour to light them, an hour to turn them out and a couple of hours to clean them, and that was his day's work. Once or twice I went with him. When he cleaned the lamps he used to have to have a ladder and I used to give him a help to carry the ladder. If't bobby saw us coming and we were walking on the causeway he used to make us go in the road. He wouldn't let you walk on't causeway with a ladder. Bobbies knew me dad, they all called him Joe.

It was Council work—those workers were devils! My uncle Bill, from across the road, he were one of them, same as me dad. He used to go around Kelvin and that area. If he'd had too much beer one day, he used to come to me brother, older than me and he'd go and do the round for him. My uncle never bothered like, used to give me brother a couple of bob for doing it.

Upstairs downstairs

My mother worked for Chesterman's who had a really big house at the side of the Botanical Gardens. They had fourteen or sixteen maids who lived in and my mother used to bring all the servants' uniforms home to wash. We lived in a yard and she used to be terrified when she hung them out to dry in case somebody muckied them.

Chesterman's had another big house in the country, and my mother used to go there for two or three months every year with a lot of servants, to spring clean. While she was away I used to go to Conisborough Childrens' Convalescent Home, just near the bottom of the Castle. When I was young I was always in and out of hospital, with eczema and my eyes. I don't think my mother paid for me to go— I think it was Chesterman's. We slept in a dormitory, about twenty of us, and we were well fed. It was alright, I used to like going. I looked forward to it because it was like going on a holiday and there was always someone you knew. They used to take you round in one of those go-carts, a pony and trap that held four. They'd take us to the station for an hour every other day and we liked looking at the trains. I think the drivers knew us eventually. We played out on the grass a lot at the home—there were big grounds. Sometimes I was a bit homesick, but not much because I knew my mother was not at home. My older brother used to come on the bus to see me every Saturday, all the way from Sheffield. I went to the Home for about ten or twelve years.

A *table-knife buffer*

When I was young you could get jobs easily and I went to work at Needham's straight from school. I lived in Dunn Street in Shalesmoor, and the place was in Henry Street, just across the road. Labour was cheap, 7/6d was top rate for a lad and if you asked for a raise they'd give you sixpence. Mind you sixpence was worth having in those days.

I was a table-knife buffer, that's not a woman's job, they did the spoons and forks. There was no apprenticeship, you just started, it was very dirty work. The grinders never wore masks to keep out the dust and they all had consumption. On Mondays the ones I worked with spent all day in the boozer and then had to make up the hours in the rest of the week. They used to go to the Wellington which was just down the street, but as I wasn't old enough to go, I had to stay and clean up. The owner of the firm, Ginger Needham, was a bit of a character. He just used to come in the office and look round a bit but he'd have the staff running the 'shop'. But he liked to be in the Wellington boozer as well!

Joe Lynch
(Aged 75)

Playing for Sheffield Wednesday

After I left school at fourteen I never kicked a football again until I was eighteen and began playing with the local lads at Pelaw. But, within six months, I was down here playing for Sheffield Wednesday—their scouts had been up north. I still remember getting off the train at the Midland Station in 1936, and how I nearly walked across the platform to catch a train back again, because I thought it was an awful place. It was the smog you know, the colour was terrible. They took me to Hillsborough via Penistone Road and it all looked a bit rough because I was used to being near the seaside where it was lovely and clear. But although I really did think it was an awful place then, I've been here ever since, and soon I'll have been married to a girl from Leppings Lane for fifty two years.

He'd been one of Sillitoe's boys

The first lodgings the club found me were with Mr and Mrs Bolsover and their daughter Ida, in Rockley Road near the ground. Mr Bolsover had been one of Sillitoe's boys, the police who got rid of the gangs and cleaned up Sheffield, but he'd been retired for a good many years when I knew him. He was a huge fellow, weighed about thirty stone, and when he sat in his easy chair he completely filled it. He wasn't satisfied with just a pint of beer at the side of him, he had a quart. It was delivered by Thompson's, the beer-off on Penistone Road. They delivered all over Sheffield in those days. We were very well fed there, and I only left because I wanted to share with three of the other boys, on Middlewood Road, just opposite the park. I was quite pally with one of the lads at that time.

Had to be back by ten-thirty

After that, we moved to Crofton Avenue, off Middlewood Road, on New Year's Eve, and that's where I met my wife, she was a friend of the landlady. Lo and behold, she came to the house and met me! That's nearly sixty years ago. Her name was Elsie Fish, her father was a shoemaker with a shop on Leppings Lane and another West Bar way. Heinz had a factory round there and his place was opposite. When we went out to the pictures and so on, we always had to be back by ten-thirty—all the young players had to. It was just the same on Saturdays after the match. The manager and trainers would drive round the streets checking up on us.

60

I'd been playing left-half for Wednesday for two or three years when I had a bad accident, cartilage, and had two operations on it. Nowadays it's simple to put right but at that time it wasn't. I did play a bit afterwards, but not much—I was born sixty years too soon.

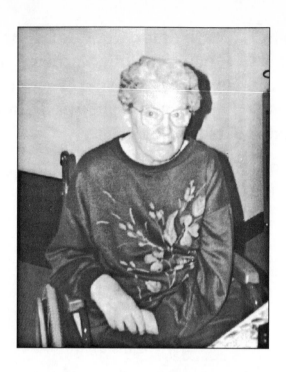

Iris Campbell
(Aged 73)

Two Iris Campbells

Years ago we went round a museum in York and we were just walking round the garden part when I saw some flowers in the distance. When we got to them I saw it was a clump of irises and they were called *Iris Campbell*—well that's my name! When we got back home I told my son we'd seen some flowers with my name on. He's bought me some since and I've got them in the back garden.

There are some funny-sized people

I went to Whitby Road School—it's still there—and my son went there as well, until he moved to High Storrs. A very good school Whitby Road, with a good reputation. I was fourteen when I left. I went straight into dressmaking, my mother had to pay for me for two years. Do you remember Roberts Bros and T. & J. Roberts used to be in town? Well I went to T. & J. Roberts. I've made most of my own clothes since I was fourteen, not this sort of thing [track suit] but dresses, jackets and skirts. I made trousers for my son when he was little and I've made trousers for men. My husband was very short-legged and could never get anything off the peg, so I made his. I've always had my own machine.

I did dressmaking before the war and I've done some since. During the war, well for nine years, I was a shop assistant at British Home Stores. I loved it there, they were lovely people to work for. Just before mother died I saw this job in the paper for an alteration-hand at Hayman's on Pinstone Street, so I rang up and the manageress said come and see me. So I did and got the job and stayed about four years—it was nice. Funny things happen sometimes, you can put zips and seams in upside down and there are some funny-sized people! You almost re-make some things. They made a lot of bridal things at Hayman's. Sometimes we had to copy things or sometimes use the customer's own design. I did some of the cutting-out as well as sewing. Later I did some dressmaking from home, but it got to be too much. My husband and son objected to these people having to come visiting for fittings, even though there weren't many of them. The house wasn't big enough, only two up and two down, but I did miss doing it. I'd do it now if I could, but I can't with this arm.

We do have some laughs

My son always helps me to get upstairs. He takes me in my chair to the bottom of the stairs, then transfers me to the lift and then there's another chair waiting at the top of the stairs—a very tall one. I've had some lovely stuff to help me from Redvers House. The Occupational Therapist, the district one, she got me a special chair for the bath. You just press a button to go up or down, which is smashing. I can have the bath nurse now. There's a concertina thing that's sat on the chair and it won't go on unless there's at least six inches of water in the bath. Sometimes she gets the hose trapped underneath it and it refuses to go then. We have some great laughs with the bath nurse, she's a lovely girl. There have been times when it's just not gone at all and she couldn't get me out of the bath. So what she's had to do, is take her shoes off and stand at the bottom of the bath, she wraps me in a big towel and then calls my son. He gets hold of me under the arms from the back and she works from the front and between them they get me out. We do have some laughs! When she's putting my clothes on she'll say, 'Come on, knickers now' and I say 'and knickers to you, too'. She says she always comes to us for a laugh and a cup of my son's coffee. She picks my embroidery up everytime she comes and says 'This isn't done yet. Come on, chop chop'. It makes my day when she comes, I'm a chatterbox, I never know when to stop. The doctor often says to me, 'Now that's enough, take a breath'. I've had some smashing doctors too.

Eric Awdas
(Aged 86)

Open until ten at night

I was born in Sheffield and went to King Edward VII school. My parents paid for me, and although we weren't really very well off, compared with a lot of people in Sheffield in those days, we were comparatively so. Then I did a three-year apprenticeship in dispensing at a privately owned chemist, going to night school and college, and that was that. I picked up a lot whilst I was working of course. Then I went to work in Portland near Weymouth for twelve months and then on to Eastbourne for another year.

When I came back to Sheffield I worked at Williams', a chemist's shop at the bottom of Fitzwilliam Street, on the corner. Although I was employed as a dispenser I helped to sell other stuff as well, fancy goods, perfume sprays and such. On Christmas Eve, for instance, we'd be open until ten at night. The shop was bombed during the war.

Then I applied for a job at Boots the chemist and went to Nottingham for an interview. They asked all sorts of questions and religion played a large part in working for that firm. The man who interviewed me was a real christian, and that helped me get the job as I've always been a churchgoer. I was placed at the Heeley Bridge shop which was later to be bombed of course. So then I went to one on Abbeydale Road and that was bombed too! They were also closing down some of the little branches which were not doing much trade. They had to find me a job as my shop had gone, so I was put on doing holiday relief and so on. I think the only shop I never worked in was the branch in High Street, but I did do fire-watching there at the beginning of the war. Did I enjoy my work? Oh yes I did, although it was tiring, such long hours. We'd work from eight or eight-thirty to eight at night and until nine on Saturdays. We had a half-day on Thursdays.

Some ipecacuahna

In those days all the drugs were loose, things such as sweet nitrate—you never hear of that now. I had a bit of a flair for mixing things together. People might ask us to mix them a bottle of cough mixture for instance, so we'd use a bit of liquorice, some ipecacuahna and so on. We'd sell menthol crystals so people could put a pinch in some boiling water for inhaling, like Friar's Balsam you know. Customers would often ask us to mix something for them in those days, or they might possibly have a doctor's prescription. We had to ring the doctors up quite a lot because it was impossible to read their writing. In either case, the medicine would always have to be paid for. The price depended on what went into each thing and we had to work out the cost of the drugs used, plus a fee for mixing. It was all extra work. There were very few ready-made tablets at that time so we made our own using a pestle and mortar, which was a very tedious job.

We had a poison cupboard

Laudanum? No, we didn't use that much as it was a very dangerous drug and was kept under lock and key. There were a lot of things kept like that, including many patent medicines. We had a poison cupboard too. Distalgesic tablets, for instance, would be kept in the poison cupboard but not under lock and key. But pharmacy work isn't what it was and there's nothing much to mix any more as medicines are mainly in tablet form. In the old days we'd have all sizes of bottles and corks, but you can't buy a cork nowadays. If the medicine is a liquid, the bottle will have a screw cap. Well, you see, it's all pills now and the chemists don't have to make anything up—only count pills.

Gordon Edy
(Aged 69)

What's in a name?

I was born in Petre Street. Father was a butcher and made me into a butcher too. When my grandfather died, scratching amongst his possessions, they came across his birth certificate and they found out that the family name wasn't *Edy* at all. Well it was, but it was *Eadie*. Grandfather was not an intellectual. He was a gravedigger in Burngreave cemetery and I suppose we must say he was illiterate. When the children were born he went down and registered them and he just said *Edy* and that's what they put down. I never liked being a butcher, but by the time I joined Father we moved and he bought another shop in Abbey Lane.

We all joined up together

I played with Millhouses Football Club. We all joined up together, when we were seventeen, all the lot of us—thirteen—all bang, bang, bang! Unfortunately thirteen of us joined up but only three of us got demobbed. Being a bit stupid, which you are at seventeen, we found out that if you went onto aircraft carriers and submarines you got 1/6d a day extra pay. If you joined up in the Air Force and went Air Crew you got 2/6d a day extra and so we all joined up Air Crew. At that time, at the beginning of the War, we took a bit of stick. We didn't stay together, we got separated. I went to America and was in the American Air Force for a year training. Then I came back to this country and into the Air Force proper.

You can get used to being shot at but . . .

I was a pilot. It was a bit of a sobering performance, because the very first raid was to Cologne and the navigator didn't return. He got killed, which brings you down to earth with a bump. So you decide it's quite a serious business this, you can get used to being shot at, but you never grow to like it. I flew Lancasters and did thirty sorties. I broke my engineer's leg! Did rather a rough landing—mind you we'd only got two engines left—so he broke his leg and we had to have a new engineer.

When I'd finished operating I spent two years instructing on Lancasters and then, because we were short of aeroplanes, I moved over to Stirlings but I wouldn't have liked to have flown Stirlings.

Elizabeth Archer
(Aged 84)

Mother didn't work—Dad wouldn't let her

Dad was an electrician. We didn't have electric lights in our house, we had gas mantles, but Dad was an electrician for Camel Laird's. Mother didn't work—Dad wouldn't let her! She had been a turner and wanted to carry on working, but one day she came home and found Dad sitting in the chair. He said that there weren't going to be two of them working, if she went out he was going to stop at home. It wasn't necessary for her to work, we could manage financially without. Mother was a very good manager, particularly with food. We used to have ham shanks, sheeps' heads, pigs' trotters and things like that. I loved sheeps' head and the brains mashed up with carrots and turnips. I like tripe, too, but I've only ever eaten it cold with salt and vinegar. I'm the only one in the family who will eat it, but I love it. Mother used to bake all her own bread too. She baked it all at home, but her Christmas cake she used to take to the back of the pork butcher's shop and he would bake it for her.

On the monkey run

I met my husband on the 'monkey run' at Handsworth. On Sunday nights we used to parade up and down at the old Handsworth terminus or sometimes we'd go to the one at Firth Park. But John lived at Darnall and I lived at Staniforth Road and we met on the Handsworth one. I was with a friend who'd met him before—a gang of them often went to the pictures together—and she took me to have a word with him. It's funny it all started from there. I'd seen him around for years but he'd never taken any notice of me before. We've had a happy marriage.

Everything just as I wanted it

We were married at Handsworth Church. It should have been the one at Attercliffe, on the main road. That was a lovely church, beautiful inside but it got blitzed. There was only the vicarage and the churchyard left. We got blitzed too, we lost our home, everything. My brother took us in and we lived up Wadsley Bridge for a bit. I had a white wedding, even though it was war time, with everything just as I wanted it. I had a long white satin dress, which I had to keep at home until the wedding because the lady who made it was frightened of being blitzed too. A lady on

Greenland Road said I could set off for my wedding from her house, because I'd no home to go from and so we kept the dress there. I had three bridesmaids. One used to work with me and the other two were daughters of the lady who looked after my wedding dress. I had pink and white carnations and the bridesmaids had daffodils, all wired —they were lovely, they came from a shop near the Pavilion on Attercliffe. The meal was difficult because of saving coupons, other people gave us coupons to help—but it wasn't really what I wanted. However, we did have a proper wedding cake, two tiers, it was lovely. The lady who looked after my dress made it. We managed some photos too, but in those days they were black and white. The bridesmaids had to be available straight away because John was in the Army and I had no idea when he would be able to come home. We married on a forty-eight-hour leave. We only had that one day together and then he had to go back. He did six years in the Army altogether. It's a big slice out of your lives.

Dad was never the same afterwards

It was terrible when we were blitzed. We were in the shelter when the landmine fell and we were able to rescue one or two things but it wasn't safe to go right inside. It finished my father off. The shock was so bad he was never the same afterwards, he started with cancer. He was working on nights that night and when he was walking home on Staniforth Road a policeman said to him, 'Don't go up there, it's all wiped out'. He came up anyway and found us all in the shelter. When we came out my mother said, 'Oh my house, my house is on fire'. But we could see right through it and it was another house that was burning that an incendiary had set fire to.

A six-roomed house for thirty pounds

While we were with my brother, some friends of ours said another friend was selling his home up because his wife had died and would we like to take it. We said yes and we got everything, a six-roomed house, fully furnished, for thirty pounds! It was near Attercliffe Palace, on Baker Street. There was a bank at one corner and a doctor's at the other. It was the third house down and it was a lovely house. They wouldn't let me have my name in the rent book, so my mother had to have it, but we paid for it. So, we had them living with us and my invalid sister too from her being seventeen to fifty-seven.

They couldn't believe it was Attercliffe

I used to love doing outside—gardening. My husband made his own in the yard, we had a big conservatory and a greenhouse as well. He grew tomatoes and the first year we had one hundred pounds, we did so well! The vicar used to say 'When I hear people say they can't grow flowers I bring them up your yard to see yours, to see what can be done'. We had tubs and all round the yard was a little wall with privet behind it. He did it for all the four houses in the yard and I did all the fronts. The last ten years or so that we were down there it improved a lot, it wasn't so dirty. We had lots of photos of that yard and garden and when I've shown them people since they've said 'Did you live there, where's that'? They couldn't believe it was Attercliffe, they thought Attercliffe was such a dump.

She did her share

It was my sister who led us to going to Wisewood, because we needed a toilet downstairs for her. She only lived twelve months after we moved there. She was terribly crippled with arthritis, fingers and everything, but you'd be surprised at the things she could do. Knitting—my husband bought her a knitting machine. She could do anything with her fingers, her embroidery used to be beautiful. To look at her hands you would never have believed it, she couldn't straighten them out, in fact we used to have to wash between her fingers with a toothbrush—but she was always happy and laughing. My children used to sit round her and she'd tell them stories and they always brought their homework to her because she was pretty clever. She did her share in the home in a different way. I couldn't get through all the work there was to do. There weren't these modern machines and it was hard work. In those days it was peg legs, tub and mangle, not an automatic machine like I had later on. Blackleading too, we were only talking about it the other day and people doing steps with donkey-stone. As soon as it rained it needed doing again.

Albert Himsworth
(Aged 77)

Sat in the tram-lines

I went to Philadelphia School. I loved school so much I ran away the first day! I went and sat in the middle of the tram-lines and I wouldn't shift. They had to fetch the police to move me and then they took me to Burgoyne Road Police Station. I was sat on the sergeant's desk when me mother came to collect me—I remember that as plain as if it were yesterday. After that I loved it! Lessons? I enjoyed 'em, I ended up getting a merit certificate for all the lot. I was recommended for High School, but the one I was recommended for you had to wear uniform and me parents couldn't afford it, so I didn't go.

In the Army now!

I joined up when I was seventeen in 1932. In 1929 when I was fourteen, the day after I left school, I went to join up. 'How old are you?' 'Eighteen Sir' I said. 'No you're not, you can't have been left school a couple of months. Anyhow, we're not recruiting for boys and we're not recruiting for men, so I can't take you'. When I was fifteen I went up again, told the same tale. Same excuse, we're not recruiting. When I was sixteen, same again. I went on my seventeenth birthday and said I was eighteen! This time it was 'We're still not recruiting for men and you are too old for boys'. I said 'Well, that's a bright thing, in't it'? He said 'Tell you what, I don't really think you are eighteen, but we'll compromise. When we do start recruiting, I'll send for you'. He never asked for my birth certificate. A couple of months later I got a paper to call in.

I called for my mate, a school pal. He was all for joining up, 'Come on Stan, they're recruiting'. We both went up to Surrey Street. We had to go upstairs for a medical examination, I went up first and passed. Then we had a scholarship, a test, and I passed that too. I signed on the dotted line and was told the pay was three shillings and fourpence a day—that was a day's pay, and one shilling and fourpence ration allowance. This was on a Friday and I was given a ten-bob note to cover three days pay. I'd never seen so much money in my life. I pocketed it and asked 'Is that it?' 'Yes, you're in the Armed Forces now'. I told them I was going home to tell my mother I'd joined up and I knew I'd cop it. I was asked to call my mate Stan upstairs, but when I looked over the bannister and shouted him, there was no one there! He'd gone back home. I broke my journey going home to call in at their house—he only lived round the corner. In I went. 'Now then Stan, I thought you were going to join up with me?' 'No, I changed my mind.' 'Well, tha's left me in't cart, an't tha?' I was right about mother, too, she played hell with me, said she'd have me out for joining under age.

The following Monday I went off to the depot and I'd just about finished my training when one day the RSM came on to the square and said that I was wanted in the CO's office. I got permission to fall out and off I went to the CO's office. I was called in and told to sit down.

'How old are you?'

'Eighteen Sir.'

'I don't think you are.'

'I know I am, Sir. I was born in 1914 on the 14th March.'

'You're sure?'

'Yes Sir.'

'I don't think you are. I think you're seventeen.'

'I don't care what you think, I know what I am—I'm eighteen.'

'You know where you are, don't you?'

'Yes Sir, in the Army.'

'Right. Well joining up under age is a criminal offence. Now I'm going to ask you a question and I want a truthful answer. How old are you?'

'Eighteen Sir.'

'I wanted a truthful answer.'

'Yes Sir, eighteen Sir.'

Then he reached under his desk and brought out a piece of paper. It was my birth certificate! Born March 14th 1915! Mother had written to claim me out for being under age.

'So how old are you?'

'Seventeen Sir. Am I going to cop for it?'

It's just an earthquake!

In 1935, the year Sheffield Wednesday won the Cup, I was in an earthquake in Quetta. That's on the North-West Frontier, India, at the foot of the Himalayan Mountains. I was only nineteen. We used to have metal plates fastened on a nail at the head of our beds and you can imagine thirty of them in a line when the earthquake happened. It started with a gentle wind, or what appeared to be a wind and the noise grew to a great crescendo, like a roll of drums. It made these brass name plates first tinkle and then get louder and louder. Then it happened. The building moved and then stopped. Nowt fell down, it was just that quick. A young soldier who'd just come out of England said 'What's that?' 'Oh, it's nowt to worry about, nowt to worry about. It's just an earthquake' But I was as terrified as him—it was my first earthquake too!

I finished my seven years, went home on St Swithin's day and forty days later I was back in again because war was declared! I didn't do any on reserve. I volunteered for this and volunteered for that. But no, I was one of the senior NCOs in the Battalion and so I was attached to the depot for training militia men and conscripts, for the duration of the war, I was told. I didn't want that. I wanted to get to France. I discovered another bloke, a corporal, who was due to be drafted to France and he didn't want to go because he was a married man with three kids. So we went together to see the CO to see if he would transfer us. He did and I ended up in a prison camp for five years! I was captured on May 30th and released on May 1st five years later.

What a waste of good treacle!

After the war, tobacco and cigarettes were scarce and rationed. I went round Woolworth's one day and I was looking at garden seeds when I spotted a packet that said 'Virginia Tobacco'. So I bought a packet and planted the seeds at the bottom of the garden. They came up lovely, really big leaves. After they got ripe, I cut the leaves off, threaded them together with cotton and hung them on the clothes line. For a while I didn't notice that they had gone from the line. Suddenly one day I said to my wife 'Now then, where are they'? 'They're in the back garden covered in cabbage leaves. Bloody tobacco!' So I fetched it all out and dusted it off. Then I sandwiched it all together with black treacle and flattened it between two boards, with holes at each end for a screw and wing nut. I put it in the airing cupboard for five or six weeks, then screwed it tighter and left it for another three months. When I eventually took it out it was as solid as a table top and I couldn't cut it, but I did manage to break a bit off. I rubbed it up and put it in my pipe—it was horrible! At work the next day I talked to Fred, an old man in my work gang and at dinner time I gave him a pipeful. He enjoyed it and asked if I'd got any more! But what a waste of good treacle!

Louie Hague
(Aged 69)

We were happy enough

The house where I was born at Hillsborough Corner is still there. I was one of twenty-three children, three of whom were already married when I was born. A lot of the twenty-three survived to grow up, and some lived into their eighties. My father was a furnaceman, but there was a lot of people out of work and we were very, very poor, but we were happy enough. Every Monday morning I used to go to the pawnshop taking clothes, which my mother had washed up over the weekend, and then I'd go to fetch them out on Friday if we'd got enough money. We all had to do some share of the housework every day, so we never had time for hobbies. Scrubbing, cleaning, mixing bread up, making beds. You didn't only have to scrub clothes outside, you had to turn them and scrub inside—because of the sweat you see. My brothers were in steel works and my mother would say 'Scrub under their arms'!

The pictures twice a day

When I was younger, before I married, I used to go to the pictures twice a day when I'd got the money. I'd go to the first house at one cinema, and the second house at another. There were plenty of picture palaces to choose from—Hillsborough Kinema in Proctor Place, the Phoenix Hillsborough

Park Cinema, Unity, Dome—plenty. I'd still like to get out like that if I was well enough. I like dancing, but my mother would never let us go, she didn't think it was the thing. She was strict with us, and she had to be, with all that lot of us.

Ten pounds compensation

I did all sorts after I left school. My first job was as a file cutter at the English Steel Corporation on Holme Lane. My mother knew the gaffer, that's how I got in, and that's where I had this finger end off. You had to put the file on the machine to cut it and the machine had a guard on, where the cogs were. Anyway, I'd got a lot of grease on my hands and I put my hand on it like this, and it slipped into the cogs. I was talking—I suppose I shouldn't have been gossiping there—and it's much it wasn't all my hand. I got ten pounds compensation. I was only fourteen and I suppose ten pounds would have been worth much more than it is now.

I liked vanillas best

When I was sixteen I started work in the bakehouse of the Don Bakery and stayed there a long time. I did everything, just worked from bench to bench doing different sorts of baking. Yes, I did eat the stuff we made, but it wasn't very good. Once a week, on Fridays, we could get things cheap. They made everything but I liked vanillas best, and custards. Nowadays I like pork pie better! I worked there up to my marriage and after.

Hygiene became very strict because Marks and Spencer used to get a lot of stuff from there, and they were ever so strict, them. You couldn't just put a hairnet over your hair, you had to have a hat right over the top and cover up every hair on your head. Well, I refused. I said 'No, I'm not going to look a fool for you, or Marks and Spencer, or nobody else. I've got a net right over the front and no hair can come out'. But anyway I left—he said I'd got to cover it up and that was it.

Sixty hours a week for three pounds

During the War I worked on munitions, drill cutting. I did what they call fluting, that's putting the flute down them. I liked doing that. I used to do twelve hours a night, sixty hours a week, from seven to seven. I got three pounds a week which was a standard wage. When there were air raids we used to go to the shelter at the back of the place until the 'all clear', when we started work again. At that time I was very fit and never needed a lot of sleep, so instead of sleeping during the day, I used to go out a lot because I knew I shouldn't be going out at night. I didn't do much, just walked round more than anything. At odd times I'd go down town to the pictures in the afternoon but not often. I was still living at home, but I was courting by then. I met my husband in the Burgoyne Pub on the top road, and we used to go in there a lot, at least when we'd got some money, he was on nights too.

One of those wind-up gramophones

We got married during the war, forty-eight years ago, but because we couldn't afford a white wedding, I wore a checked two piece, but no hat—I don't like hats. We didn't have a wedding cake either, but we had jam and lemon tarts at a party at my home. There was a good crowd and it was alright. There was one of those wind-up gramophones with a horn and it was a full-time job keeping it going. Everybody tried to dance, but there really wasn't much room for that.

No more Apperknowle

My husband used to play football for Johnny Ward's where he worked in the rolling mills. The firm was at Malin Bridge, just up Loxley New Road. Was he good at football? Well, he thinks he was, but I don't know because I've never understood it. He played cricket for them as well. Once he went to Apperknowle for a match and he didn't come back until ever so late at night. When he got back I said 'Where've you been 'til this time'? He said 'Playing cricket' and I said 'You're the only bloody firm that plays in the dark, and anyway, there'll be no more Apperknowle'.

Nelly Thickett
(Aged 82)

Samples of silver to Mappin and Webb

When I was the chief cabinet case liner with E. Greaves & Son, with eight girls under me, Mr Geoffrey, the fourth son I think he was, used to come to me for whatever was needed. We used velvet and silk, lovely materials which I would never have been able to buy for myself. The cases, folders we called them, were used by travellers to take samples of silver and stuff to firms like Mappin and Webb and so on. No two were ever alike and I had to be careful because of the different sizes. I left because I'd had enough as I'd worked there from leaving school until I was in my thirties. Mr Geoffrey died of cancer recently. He was a millionaire and they couldn't save him, and now they reckon the firm's up for sale.

No grants or anything else

I was a widow, probably in my forties, when I began to run my rest home which I called 'Marguerite'. It was two houses put together, on Upper Albert Road at Heeley Green, with us living in one and using the other for the Home. It's still there, being run by two doctors now but I expect the prices have shot up! I only charged enough to pay Gwen, my helper, and myself a wage but I didn't want to make a profit. There were just the two of us working there. I had it nicely decorated and so on, but the only money I got was from the people who stayed with me—no grants or anything else.

Tha cooks me a good dinner lass

We could take up to a dozen, so that the carers could have a rest while we looked after their relatives for a fortnight. We'd wash them, give them baths, do everything. The doctors said we shouldn't lift them as it was heavy work, but we did. I'm regretting that now though! I used to cook as well, and Gwen would say, 'Tha cooks me a good dinner lass'. She'd help me wash up and so on. Gwen was local, from the Park district, and she was very good. I've not seen her for quite a bit though. Did I tell you I called the house 'Marguerite'—my daughter's called Margaret, I do wish she'd come while you're here as she's a very nice person. She'd do anything for anybody.

Ted Walker

(Aged 84)

A right red nose

I never went to school much. My mother or my grand-mother used to take me to school, in through one gate and I used to get out of the back gate as fast as I could. Sometimes I used to go fishing up to Rivelin—it only cost a ha'penny on the tram. Eventually my mother found out because the school people asked her why I wasn't going to school. It didn't make a lot of difference though.

I didn't like school and I didn't like the teachers. One of them had a right red nose and he often ended up at the back of the blackboard drinking whisky. Another one had a stick nine or ten inches long and about two inches thick. You used to get your name in the punishment book and then have to go in front of him and he used to stroke it on your hand. I ended up in the same standard as I started in I think. I did learn to read and write though.

Emily Cowlishaw
(Aged 85)

I made half my wedding dress!

I made half my wedding dress! The woman I was working for promised to make it but she'd only half done it when she found she was too busy to finish it, so I did the rest. It was white with a close-fitting bodice and a big train with lace straps round the bottom edge. Six of my friends were bridesmaids because I couldn't leave any of them out, and I think they wore pink. I still have my veil and my shoes too, they were white satin but rather clumpy in design at that time—nowadays they'd be court shoes. You know, we've been married fifty odd years now, and never had any serious upsets.

All that washing and ironing

My husband had an office job, because he didn't want farming and his uncle took that over. Just after we were married he got a management post and was earning a very good wage in comparison with many people. We had a house in the Norfolk Park area, which was lovely then, all green fields and the walk to town down Granville Road was so picturesque. We lived in a period house and I polished everything in sight just as my mother did. For a while I made clothes for my daughters, until they wanted all the latest styles. Do you know, I don't think they've ever picked a needle up!

I used to embroider tablecloths and cushion covers, in fact everything was embroidered within an inch of its life! I've still got plenty of tablecloths but they're falling apart now—all that washing and ironing. No, I don't know if they'll be heirlooms because younger people tend not to want what you like do they?

Margery Searle
(Aged 84)

Those were the days!

I was born in Sussex, in a country place called Midhirst
and lived there until I started my nursing training in Eastbourne. I worked in London mainly and then retired with
a friend to Kent. Unfortunately, she died, and my sister,
who lives up here said, 'You can't stay down here on your
own'. So, they brought me up here and we bought a bungalow together—she and her husband are so good to me.
In fact Sheffield has been very good to me because I'm a
stranger here and they give me all I can want. I don't think
they are as generous down South, well I haven't found
them so.

I had to do two years nursing training in Eastbourne and then another two years in Lambeth in London. I was very, very lucky because I was the only probationer they had had for six months—nobody wanted me to start with! But the other end of the programme was good because I was the senior nurse for six months. I had all the theatre work and that sort of thing. We didn't think the training was too hard, we all shared it alike and we had nothing to compare it with, we were quite happy, as I got to know more about the work I really enjoyed it.

We had one day off a month and one pound pay per month. Uniform, with starched cuffs and high collars, and food and lodging were provided of course, but we were never allowed out after ten at night. The Mayor of Eastbourne provided the nurses with a bathing hut and we had freedom of the tennis courts or we went walking. We never had any money and we didn't see much of our families. When one of the girls wrote home she never put a stamp on the envelope! We had good food and we were well looked after. I remember one Christmas I had a parcel from Mother and as I told Cook what I'd got in it, one of the Sisters came up and said, 'You don't think you're going to starve, do you'? Mother thought I was, though!

We wore starched caps with strings, like Florence Nightingale, for special occasions or just a clip for normal duty, they stayed in place quite well. We didn't have to launder our uniforms, it was done for us. Our frocks came down to our ankles and our starched aprons came right round us with straps that crossed at the back. The frock sleeves were long and we had starched cuffs to go over them. Junior nurses wore striped blue and senior nurses plain blue. There were stoves to heat the wards in those days, not central heating and patients didn't get up and sit round a table for meals, it was always trays on the bed. You had to have a secondary school education to be a nurse in those days—a certain standard of education before you were accepted.

'Now you can finish off your job'

When I first started nursing I was really green you know. They put me on a male ward but I wasn't very good. I was running round from pillar to post getting nowhere. One morning I thought, I'll really get everything done today— my mother was a real tartar for getting everything clean, which was good training for me—so I worked hard, finished all my jobs and was ready to go off duty from twelve noon until two pm when Home Sister arrived to do a ward round. She said, 'Where do you think you are going to'? I said, 'I'm off duty, Sister'. 'Oh,' she said, 'we'll see if you've done it all or not then'. She didn't bother to see, everything went in the bath or the sluice with the water turned on. Then she went round the ward and put everything on the floor. 'Now' she said, 'You can finish off your job'. I hadn't been there more than a fortnight! I went straight on and did everything again, because you never argued in those days. I put all the lockers right, cleaned the bed pans and things again and re-stacked everything. It was almost two o'clock when I'd finished. Home Sister never did that to me again, but it did upset me at the time. They put me on a female ward soon after that and I was quite happy when I'd got over it.

I was proud

I took my State Registration after I'd finished my two years in London and then did an extra year for my midwifery. I had a good time, delivered some babies in their homes, others in hospital and then went on the district for quite a while, but not as a midwife, even though I did the training. I found district nursing more interesting. When I sat my midwifery exam I thought 'Oh, I've failed' 'cos the examiner never seemed to pass anyone from my hospital. She was a tartar really. We had to write a paper first and then had an oral afterwards. When I saw her I thought 'Lor, I'm for it'! But I answered as best I could and then she enquired about the paper I'd done. When it came to, I was the only nurse in that Lambeth hospital to be passed by her. I *was* proud! When we did our preliminary exam in Eastbourne, Matron took so many into her room to start with, to give us the results, and I was one of the ones left outside. I thought I'd failed then too, but it turned out she'd spoken to the failures first and I'd passed.

I was in London throughout the War. It was terrible. When we were on night duty, we'd go home not knowing whether it was still there or not. One morning I went home and both corners of the road had gone, we had a flat at that time. Under the Underground stations they built small shelters and put in bunks and we used to go, once a week, on duty as nurses, we helped those who were hurt in the air raids. I remember one night a bomb came down on where people were being sorted out to go to various places. They'd lost their homes already and were just waiting to be helped, and then that happened to them. It was awful. When the raids were a little less they used to put up the men who were coming home on leave, just overnight, before they travelled on. We had great fun then really.

I started nursing at nineteen and continued until I was fifty and then I went to work in Boots, the chemists. I started with rheumatism you see, and all the standing with nursing was too much. This was easier and regular hours—very nice. I gave nursing advice, often for customers' children, but I used to serve on the counter too, and fit things like elastic stockings. I always tried to direct people to their doctor if I felt they needed more than simple remedies. First of all I worked in the Brixton shop and then transferred to Streatham, which was a bigger shop and I finally retired at sixty.

Sydney Pearson
(Aged 80)

'Let me be your father'

I went to Owler Lane School which was only a few minutes' walk away, and then at twelve I got a scholarship to the Pupil Teachers Centre, next door to the Central School, in Holly Street. Did I enjoy it? Well as much as any kid enjoys school, and of course I had to travel backwards and forwards to town every day. I left school during the depression, and got a job with the Bennett Correspondence Course College, in their offices at Melbourne Avenue. I stayed there for about three years, checking papers that their students were sending in, exam papers and so on. It wasn't a bad job but it wasn't very well paid. The college advertised a lot, their maxim being Mr Bennett saying 'Let me be your father'.

I'd titivate myself up

When I was about seventeen and working at Bennett's College, I met my wife. Her job there was to take the papers round to the tutors who were going to work on them. She was only a kid then and they gave her all the menial tasks, but that's how it was then, especially for girls. It shows how much I loved her because I used to go from Firvale to Crosspool, where she lived, every night. I'd titivate myself up before I left home, getting my hair right and that, but sometimes I'd play pop when I got to her house, because as soon as I got off the bus and turned on to her road there'd be a blooming wind blowing. 'I try to make myself smart to come up to see you, and that wind has messed my hair up again.' The weather seemed to be different there as it's so high up, decent at Page Hall, but by the time I got up there, nearly snowing.

Draughts from all directions

Then I went on the trams. At first I was a conductor, as you had to spend about twelve months getting experience of what to do and where to go. After that I did twenty years as a driver. It wasn't a bad job because all my mates were friendly people, but the hours, now they were pretty bad. The first trams I drove were completely open at the front but the funny thing was that they weren't half as draughty as the later ones which were enclosed, except of course for the places where people got on and off. In the early ones you had the wind coming straight at you and it sort of went past, but in the others draughts came from all sorts of directions. You didn't know where they came from but you knew where they were going to—down the back of your neck usually. But of course the last trams, the really modern ones, were a piece of cake.

We all belonged to a particular section with its own roster, and I was on the Brightside keyboard, although this didn't mean that I would be on that run all the time. You might be down to do a month perhaps on Brightside, and then for the next two months you'd be on completely different sections before you got back to Brightside again. On my rota, the first duty signed on at eight minutes past four in the morning, and I'd have to be up by three to catch the mail car to get there. I was based at Weedon Street, at Tinsley, on the early turn. This duty, which finished at just after one o'clock, was the one I preferred because I could get home, have the afternoon in bed, and then be free for the evening. On the next duty I felt that my day was wasted altogether.

Arthur Ellis

(Aged 82)

Window tapping

We even did this trick on our own homes. We had a long piece of string with a pig's trotter bone tied about a foot along the string, and a pin on the end of the string. We used to stick the pin in the window frame, let out a long length of string, get hiddied and then—tap, tap, tap, tap, tap, tap with the bone on the window. We did it for so long, then when we heard a door opening, a quick pull, the pin came out and we'd gone!

Hanging on carts

One thing that stands out in me mind was there used to be railway horses and carts, drays, and across the back of them there was an iron bar. I was hanging on there one day and got such a PLONK! at the side of me ear'ole! I thought he'd knocked me ear off. Do you know what it were? A constable's gloves! He said 'Don't let me catch you doing that anymore'.

Did you ever get the strap?

Do you know, me father made his own leather belt. It was three-inch-wide leather and three buckles to fasten it, and he could whip that off as quick as them fellers could draw a gun in't cowboys. He was just threatening, he never used it, but he frightened us to death. Me mother had a cane, one of them long thin canes with a hook on and she'd get that down and threaten us if we didn't do what we were told. I think worst punishment was to put us on't stairs and close t'door—'Stop there while you can behave yourself'—and I'd be left in the dark! They never ill-treated any of us, they were firm. If they said do a thing we had to do it.

Little boxes

I worked at Fox and Robinson's on Randall Street for forty years. They made boxes for beer, whisky and such like—crates you know. I worked on the circular saw and had many accidents—my hands are permanently damaged now. The women made light wooden boxes for Batchelor's peas. They used a machine that put in seven nails at once. I met my wife at the factory. We used to do our courting in Whiteley Woods and Tinsley Park Woods, or we'd often meet at the top of Commercial Street and go to the Electra in Fitzalan Square or to the Wicker.

Blackclocks

We got married on Boxing Day. We'd had a house at Darnall for seven weeks and we'd done it up. After we got married and had been living there for three months my wife saw all these blackclocks—it was terrible! We'd got an aunt at Carbrook who got us an exchange, because she knew some people who wanted to move to Darnall as they'd got pigeon lofts there. But, one night when we came back from the pictures we put the light on and there were more blackclocks than there'd been at Darnall! We got some stuff called Union Paste—smoke came out when you took the lid off. It was spread on six inch squares of brown paper. You never saw any dead blackclocks but they went. That stuff was used to clean up this place [Northern General] when it was the Firvale Infirmary.

Sally Fox
(Aged 86)

I looked after my things

I had a special doll that my mother bought me for Christmas, a proper one, not a wooden one. Later she bought me what would be called a carrycot nowadays—they were just little bits of things then. I had that doll for years and then I gave it to one of my nieces but she didn't have it for as many minutes as I'd had it for years! I remember a tea service—cups, saucers, teapot, milk jug, sugar basin—that I had for years, love. I looked after my things. What we had we took care of. My mother had to turn out to earn money to buy us toys.

We called our local policeman Bobby Longlegs because he was so tall. He'd hit us on the back of the neck with his gloves if we did anything wrong so that we wouldn't do it again—but we used to, love, we used to do. But, when he noticed us girls skipping with just a piece of orange box rope, he got us some proper, heavier stuff, to use instead.

Every year we had a marvellous week's holiday at Clee-thorpes, because my father had a travel pass through his work on the railways. He didn't go with us, and we were glad because he was so strict and none of us could relax when he was around. We had a very good place to stay, in the Market Place, and I loved the swimming, the ice creams, and the donkey rides.

Leg of lamb for 2/6d

You could get a leg of lamb for two shillings and sixpence —a proper leg, not what you get nowadays. My mother cooked it in an oven in the fireplace, and we'd have it for Sunday dinner. Then at night, all the family came round after they'd had a drink, and there'd be enough meat for sandwiches for tea.

On the road near us in Harvest Lane, there was a cookhouse where they made meat and potato pies. The men used to come across the road from where they worked, and they could either sit in the shop to eat their pies or take them out. All the men used to speak to us children because they saw us every day, and there was never any fear like nowadays.

When I was fourteen I went straight from school to work at a spice factory in Bridge Street. They made liquorice allsorts, aniseed balls, Pontefract cakes and 'Victory V' lozenges. We women wore overalls with trousers because we worked on the machines making 'Victory Vs'. We weren't allowed to eat the sweets but sometimes one or two just fell into our pockets!

George Brown
(Aged 67)

I love nursing

I worked at British Acheson's and was encouraged by the doctor and nurse there to do industrial nursing. I love nursing, but never thought of doing it when I left school. I worked at Sanderson Kayser's too, on Tyler Street, I was employed as an industrial nurse then. Aswell as my job, I was also doing my Red Cross work and running my concert party.

I had my own concert party

Now I've always liked entertaining people, and started when I was about thirteen. My dad did a bit of comedy like, and

I followed suit. He didn't belong to anything formal but he'd always get everybody laughing at parties, he was a character. Well I had my own concert party that I called 'George Brown's music hall', and we'd go round hospitals, homes—anywhere where they'd have us, I was the comedian. When did I start it? Now you're asking! I can't really remember.

My wife Jean and my son David, were in the show and we had four chorus girls, they were only little lasses, sixteen or seventeen years old. I used to do Hylda Baker, 'She knows you know', that's the one, and Frank Randle in the 'old hiker' sketch. When I was twenty-four, I had all my teeth out so that I could really impersonate him. Well, what's wrong with that? I just wanted to impersonate him. One year we went to the Blind Institute on Mappin Street, to do a pantomime, and gave them all the money we made. It was a hundred and sixty-something quid, and it made my day. We did Aladdin that time, I was the Emperor and my son was Wishee Washee—he was a comedian as well.

My party piece

Now I always used to play to the audience wherever I was, and I remember doing my party piece in this particular sketch. I'll never forget it. My son was all dolled up complete with dicky bow, and saying, 'Ladies and gentlemen I am going to recite for you'. Then I'd come on dressed as this old caretaker, wearing a brown overall coat and a cap on the side of my head. I'd have no teeth in and I'd be carrying a mop and bucket. I'd pick on one person in the audience—and you know I should never have picked on her because she was so hoity toity—and say 'Move tha' legs, love. Let me clear it up, tha's wet all o'er'. Anyway it went on and on, and our David couldn't carry on any more for laughing. Then this fella stood up. 'Excuse me young man. We've paid good money to see this show, and we don't want an idiot like you coming in mopping up the carpet.' Everybody else howled because they knew what was going on.

Pulling Irish Mary's leg

Now, every New Year, we'd have an all-night party at home, and then I'd go on to work the morning after, giving injections and so on! At midnight we'd go out to one or two neighbours and friends, coming back at about two o'clock to carry on with the party. Now, one year I decided to play a joke on Irish Mary, one of our friends. You might have heard her on Radio Sheffield, and can she talk! We've been friends for years with her and her husband, but every time we meet, Mary and I argue. We're really good mates though. Now I'd planned to put my tramp outfit on because Mary had never seen it. I told my wife because I didn't want her to put the cat among the pigeons when I appeared. I was going to change at a neighbour's house so I just said to everybody, 'I'm just popping across the road to Amy's', she was an invalid, 'to put the light on for her and that'. Anyway, I got dressed and made up and then went to knock on my own front door and asked if George Brown was in. They said no, but I went in anyway. I sat down next to Mary, and of course, she didn't know she was the stooge. 'How do lass, are tha all right?' No answer, so I said 'I've spoken to thee and don't tha forget that tramps are worth more than any other people'. Anyway, I went on and on, and then I asked where George was, and she said he'd gone to see a neighbour. 'Ee', I said, 'tha's got a lovely leg'. Well, she was all for fetching the police by now. She's tall, about six feet, and she turned round and said, 'You can leave my legs alone. If George was here he'd have you'. So I said, 'I'm not frightened of George'. Anyway, I went on kidding her, and I could see I was winding her up, so I brought a duster out of my pocket and said, 'Do you want to blow your nose, love, before I blow mine'? That did her, 'You filthy little man, I don't know how George puts up with you', and she got me by the scruff of my neck and lifted me up, right off the ground. She was that big, she'd been a military policewoman. Anyway I just had to laugh and tell her to put me down, but she said, 'Oh no, I'm going to put you out'. Well, my mother was there at the time and she said, 'Put him down Mary, it's our George tormenting you'. 'Thank you Mother', I said, 'You've spoilt my sketch'. Anyway Mary just dropped me. Did she laugh? You know I can't remember, but I enjoyed it. I'd worked my part to make her believe I was somebody else. That's what you've got to do.

Michael Czernijewski
(Aged 76)

They have proper weather there

We lived in Posnam, Poland, one hundred miles from the German border. They have proper weather there, you know, winter is winter, and summer really is summer. I remember that winter of 1921–22 when we had four to five feet of snow between Christmas and New Year. The snow was frozen, the wind was whistling and we were sitting round our wood burning fire, then the door opened. I'll never forget what happened next.

The chap who came in had a long beard down to his waist, frozen with snow. Nobody recognised him. Not even my grandmother, his wife, recognised him. You see, in 1913–14 when the war began and Polish people were taken to Austria, Russia and Germany, my grandfather was forced into the old Russian army. Anyway, he stood inside the door for a few moments, and I remember how they all stopped talking and started jumping up and crying. Grandmother had recognised him, my mother—his sisters and brothers—all of them.

From that time Grandfather never stopped talking about it because everybody kept coming to sit round the fire to discuss it. Now what had happened was that the Russian army was so terrible that Grandfather ran off, taking one to two years to get back to Poland. There were all sorts of tales to tell. But you know, the Russians still knew all about him, because in 1945 when the Germans went out and the Russians came in, their Secret Service came to our house to ask for him. They had details of all sorts of Polish people. We said 'He is dead', but they did not believe us and asked where he was buried. Then they went to the church to check the certificates and looked for the cross in the churchyard.

In three weeks I was in the front line

In 1939 when the war broke out, all men born in 1916 were called up, and in three weeks I was in the front line. There were Germans on three sides and I don't know how I survived, but God was with me. When I became a prisoner of war I was sent to work on a farm in Germany, but the farmer was a real German, not SS. I got on well with his family, but then he was taken into the army, and the man who took his place did not like me. He told lies about me and I was put in a concentration camp. As you can guess, it was a hard life in there.

The guards used to carry enormous bunches of keys swinging from their belts, and one day one of them hit me on the forehead with his keys. I was taken to the hospital there. I had a holy medal round my neck, which was forbidden, and when the doctor came to sew up my wound I realised that he had spotted it and I was frightened to death. He whispered to me 'I am a Czech, don't be frightened, they have forced me to do this work. I will help you to survive'. Then he said 'I'll give you two tablets, painkillers, but hide them or we'll both be shot. Don't swallow or eat them, save them until the pain gets bad and just lick them a bit. Then hide them again'. I hid them in the waistband of my trousers. That doctor saved my life with those tablets. Later I saw a photo of him, and writing saying he had been shot by the Germans. I don't know if it was true—it might have been propaganda

Back to the farm

After the camp closed it was always my intention to go back to the farm. I had a big revolver, which an American had given me, hidden in my clothes. I was going back to shoot that man who had sent me to the camp. The people at the farm had never expected to see me again, they thought I'd be dead—going to that camp was like being given a death sentence. So the first thing they knew about my return was when they saw me standing there holding the gun. They were frightened that I was going to shoot them.

Anyway I asked where Fred, the bad German was. 'He's the only one in danger—I know you're innocent.' Then they told me that when the farmer came back in 1944 his wife told him how Fred had sent me to the concentration camp, so two weeks later he had Fred sent into the army, to the Eastern Front. Polish partisans shot him in December 1944. I believed what they told me and put the gun away. 'I shan't harm you. I came for him, not you.' Then the farmer's children ran up, they were just little kids, aged about seven. They used to play with me as though we were brothers, wanting me to carry them on my shoulders. I'd brought them some chocolate that the Americans had given me. They all wanted me to stay on the farm but I went after two days. You see I thought there might be trouble between Russia and the Western powers, and I wanted to get away from it all.

'What's the best paid?'

I chose to come here, to England, to Britain, and arrived in 1948. I stayed in Harwich for four weeks, there were thousands of displaced persons there—and then I was moved to Scotland. I can remember the names on the journey there—Invergordon, Inverness . . . When I was asked what job I wanted to do, farming and so on, I asked 'What's the best paid'? and it was coal mining. As I was filling in the application forms they said 'It's very dirty you know' but I didn't mind.

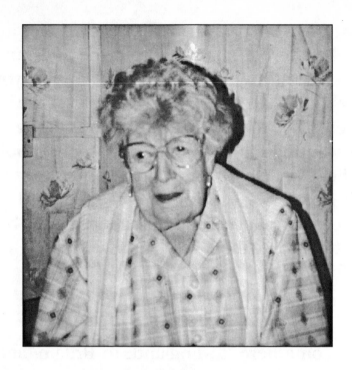

Annie Darby
(Aged 91)

Bread and dripping if we were lucky

I went to St Catherine's on Andover Street when I was four, and left at fourteen. It was run by the Catholic nuns from the convent on Burngreave Road, but there were Protestants at the school as well. Every day me and another girl had to fetch hot dinners for the nuns, in canisters from the convent kitchens, but all we had to eat was bread and dripping—if we were lucky. For school we wore white pinafores which fastened down the back. They had frills which had to be done with goffering irons that you'd warm in the fire first. We had boots which fastened using button hooks, and very thick stockings held up with elastic garters.

We were made to go to Sunday School, and I went to Burngreave Congregational at the top of Gower Street. Now, if you could say a certain number of psalms straight off, you'd get a Lord Wharton's Bible. I don't know who the Lord Wharton was—some big man I expect. I got mine in 1913. I had a Bible and a prayer book, both with pages edged with gold. I've still got them and they are as lovely as when they were new. At Whitsuntide we used to walk from the church to Firth Park, to sing following the banner. It was a long way but you could walk in those days, you were used to it. We used to go to the Band of Hope on Tuesdays, where we played and made things out of tissue paper.

Twenty-seven shillings—a millionaire

When I left school at fourteen I soon got a job as an errand girl down Orange Street, just off West Street, taking spoons and pots to different places for half a crown a week. Now, while I was running these errands, I found another job down Trafalgar Street for three shillings a week. They had a place on Division Street where they made buffs for buffers. You put a piece of cloth one way, another piece the other way, and then cut them to make rings to put on the buffs. I was doing these two jobs when I found a third, at Gills on Eyre Lane, for six shillings and sixpence a week. I remember that I had to climb a lot of steps on the outside of this place, right to the top. I was well off with these three wages.

When the 1914 War broke out, and I went to Vicker's on Brightside, I got twenty-seven shillings for sweeping up and I was a millionaire. Of course we always used to tip up to our mothers, and I got thre'pence a week spending money.

'Them were the days'

When I was married I still worked—papering, washing, all sorts. I cleaned for an old lady who was a Spirella corset maker and lived in a cellar-kitchen house down Nottingham Cliff. Them were the days! I'd do the windows, bedrooms and that for six shillings, when other people only paid three. Even when I had a full time job I'd go there on Thursdays, she wouldn't have anyone else to clean for her. I used to clean for someone on Vivian Road, who had two daughters working at Banner's at Page Hall, and her neighbour. I'd do one in the morning and the other in the afternoon. They gave me three shillings each.

Washing drying everywhere

There was a chip shop facing Sutherland Road Baths and for three shillings I'd do the family's washing. It had to be blued, starched, mangled and ironed. It *was* washing in them days! The money was paid on Saturdays and I'd use it to get a joint for Sunday. You could get a rabbit and a pound of stewing meat for 18d [1/6d] from Oliver's in Gower Street. I used to send my eldest daughter to get the money, and on this particular Saturday, Mrs Peckett, she said to our Millie, 'Tell your mother she got one of Harold's shirt cuffs dirty', so I said 'Take her bloody three shillings back and tell her to do her own washing'. Well, she came down to me roaring, but I didn't do it any more, love, we went without our Sunday dinner.